ISBN 978-1-330-53538-7
PIBN 10075198

1 MONTH OF
FREE
READING

at

www.ForgottenBooks.com

By purchasing this book you are eligible for one month membership to ForgottenBooks.com, giving you unlimited access to our entire collection of over 1,000,000 titles via our web site and mobile apps.

To claim your free month visit:

www.forgottenbooks.com/free75198

English
Français
Deutsche
Italiano
Español
Português

www.forgottenbooks.com

Mythology Photography **Fiction**
Fishing Christianity **Art** Cooking
Essays Buddhism Freemasonry
Medicine **Biology** Music **Ancient
Egypt** Evolution Carpentry Physics
Dance Geology **Mathematics** Fitness
Shakespeare **Folklore** Yoga Marketing
Confidence Immortality Biographies
Poetry **Psychology** Witchcraft
Electronics Chemistry History **Law**
Accounting **Philosophy** Anthropology
Alchemy Drama Quantum Mechanics
Atheism Sexual Health **Ancient History**
Entrepreneurship Languages Sport
Paleontology Needlework Islam
Metaphysics Investment Archaeology
Parenting Statistics Criminology
Motivational

REFERENCE TO THE PRESENT CONDITION

OF THE

UNITED STATES.

By JOEL PARKER.

CAMBRIDGE:

WELCH, BIGELOW, AND COMPANY,
PRINTERS TO THE UNIVERSITY.

1862.

CONSTITUTIONAL LAW.

[From the North American Review, for April, 1862.]

1. *The Constitution of the United States of America, with an Alphabetical Analysis; the Declaration of Independence; the Articles of Confederation; the prominent Political Acts of George Washington, &c., &c., &c.* By W. HICKEY. Seventh Edition. Philadelphia. 1854.

2. *The Federalist, on the New Constitution, written in the Year* 1788. By MR. HAMILTON, MR. MADISON, and MR. JAY. With an Appendix, &c., &c. A new Edition. Hallowell: Glazier, Masters, and Smith. 1842.

3. *Constitutional Law. Being a Collection of Points arising upon the Constitution and Jurisprudence of the United States, which have been settled by Judicial Decisions and Practice.* By THOMAS SERGEANT, Esquire. Philadelphia: Abraham Small. 1822.

4. *A View of the Constitution of the United States of America.* By WILLIAM RAWLE, LL. D. Second Edition. Philadelphia: Philip H. Nicklin. 1829.

5. *Commentaries on the Constitution of the United States; with a Preliminary Review of the Constitutional History of the Colonies and States before the Adoption of the Constitution.* By JOSEPH STORY, LL. D., Dane Professor of Law in Harvard University. Boston: Hilliard, Gray, & Co. Cambridge: Brown, Shattuck, & Co. 1833.

6. *A Course of Lectures on the Constitutional Jurisprudence of the United States, delivered annually at Columbia Col-*

lege, New York. By William Alexander Duer, late President of tiat Institution. Second Edition. Boston: Little, Brown, & Co. 1856.

7. *Speech of* Hon. M. F. Conway *of Kansas. Delivered in the House of Representatives, December* 12, 1861. Wasiington, D. C.: Scammel & Co. 1861.

8. Mr. Sumner's *Resolutions. Resolutions declaratory of the Relations between the United States and the Territory once occupied by certain States, and now usurped by pretended Governments, without Constitutional or Legal Right.* Boston: Daily Evening Transcript, February 12, 1862.

"Mr. President:— When the mariner has been tossed for many days in thick weather, and on an unknown sea, he naturally avails himself of the first pause in the storm, the earliest glance of the sun, to take his latitude, and ascertain how far the elements have driven him from his true course. Let us imitate this prudence, and, before we float farther on the waves of this debate, refer to the point from which we departed, that we may at least be able to conjecture where we now are."

Tiese memorable words of a great statesman, preliminary to tie commencement of iis magnificent reply to Senator Hayne, contain a sentiment wiici is of wide application; and in tiese days of difficulty and of trial, in whici the stormy passions and illogical arguments of ieated politicians obscure tie principles of constitutional law, and tie more insidious undercurrents of interested political aspirants are drifting us iard upon tie breakers of disorganization, tie prudence wiici tiat sentiment inculcates may well admonisi us to take a fresi observation of tiat political sun by tie aid of wiici tie siip of state must be steered, if we expect to attain tie iaven of constitutional peace.

Tie civil iistory of tie United States from tie Declaration of Independence to tie adoption of tie Constitution is one of great interest. The formation of State governments, with constitutions providing for a distribution of powers, in their nature legislative, executive, and judicial, among departments duly organized for their administration, in a manner best adapted to exemplify and enforce the great principle of self-government, by the grant of sufficient power to rulers, but with limitations necessary to the preservation and security of the rights of the people, was a problem which required and received the careful consideration of the most enlightened citizens of the several States, acting separately, and with reference to the previous laws, habits, and interests of their several communities. At the same time, the formation of a permanent confederation of the several States, with sufficient powers for the prosecution of the war, and for the promotion of the general welfare of the whole,— as associated governments, having to a certain extent a united purpose and a common interest, — tasked the energies and faculties of the eminent men who then composed the Congress of the United States.

The difficulties attending the formation of such a Confederacy, arising from the diverse, and in some respects adverse, interests of different States, were finally surmounted, and the Articles of Confederation were ratified by all the States; but it soon became apparent that the government of the Confederation was inadequate for the purposes which it was designed to subserve. There was not sufficient power to regulate the commerce of the country and to provide for the general welfare, and the conflicting interests of different States were endangering the peace and happiness of the people. Negotiations for the adjustment of some of the matters of difference resulted in the Convention which framed the Constitution. It was called for the purpose of preposing amendments to the Articles of Confederation; but it was soon admitted that the defects of the system were too great to be overcome in that mode, and that a radical change, constructing a government of tie general ciaracter of tie State governments so far as tie division and distribution of powers were concerned, but limited to tie purposes for wiici a general government was needed, was tie only effective remedy for existing evils. As tie matter for consideration was one wiici was vital to tie iappiness and prosperity of tie country, tie several States sent some of tieir most prominent men as delegates to tie Convention ; and tiis august body continued in session nearly four montis, forming and maturing tie plan, and proceeding witi tie most praisewortiy care and caution. All matters in wiich a difference of opinion existed were fully debated and considered, and tie several propositions were submitted to tie " Committee of Detail," wiici not only revised, but carefully collated and arranged, tie different parts of tie proposed instrument.

Wien tie work was completed, copies of it were furnisied to tie several States and to Congress, witi a letter in wiici are tiese significant paragrapis, viz. : " It is obviously impracticable, in tie federal government of tiese States, to secure all rigits of independent sovereignty to eaci, and yet provide for tie safety and interest of all." " In all our deliberations on tiis subject, we kept steadily in our view tiat wiich appeared to us tie greatest interest of every true American, — tie consolidation of tie Union, — in wiici is involved our prosperity, felicity, safety, periaps our national existence." Many persons feared tiat tie powers proposed to be granted were too great, and tiat tiere was danger tiat tie new government would swallow up tie State organizations, tie very tiing of all otiers wiici it was not designed to accomplisi. It underwent a most searciing and critical analysis. Messrs. Hamilton, Madison, and Jay, in a series of papers (most of wiici were written by tie two gentlemen first named) wiici iave since been collected under tie title of " Tie Federalist," and form a standard commentary on tie Constitution, gave it a very powerful support, and probably saved it from rejection.* In several of the conventions of the people of the different States to which it was submitted for ratification, there were long debates upon its general character, and upon particular parts of it, and in many it was ratified by but small majorities, mainly from the fear, before suggested, that too much of the power of the States would be surrendered by its adoption.

This brief reference to the history of the formation and ratification of the Constitution may serve to show that we should hold fast to the government which it has provided, and abide by the constitutional obligations which it imposes upon us. Surely we cannot hope that more favorable circumstances will occur for the dispassionate formation of a new Constitution, or that the construction of such an instrument will be committed to wiser or more patriotic men. If the present government is subverted, either by a secession of parts or by a usurpation of powers belonging to the States, who shall assure us that the process of disintegration, or usurpation, once begun, will not end in the entire destruction of the republic?

It would seem, at first, that the general principles of an instrument which had been subjected to such an ordeal, and to such numerous and most able expositions, must by the time it was fairly adopted have been very fully understood. But it is quite evident that the subject was not exhausted.

The compendium of judicial decisions upon different parts of the Constitution, more particularly relating to the jurisdic-

---

* In the edition of this work now in the library of the Law School of Harvard College, some unknown and unauthorized annotator has entered, in pencil, immediately before the first number, this important piece of information, viz.: " This number was written by A. Hamilton, on a small writing-desk belonging to Mrs. Hamilton, and sent to her from England by her sister, whilst on his passage up the North River in a small sloop. The authenticity of this is indisputable. Any one asking to see the desk can be accommodated at Barnum's Museum. Price, 25 cents."

We print the note for the benefit of persons curious in such matters. They can doubtless find the locality indicated!

tion and practice of the courts, by Thomas Sergeant, was published in 1822. A second edition, under a slightly varied title, with additions and improvements, appeared in 1830.

The first edition of Mr. Rawle's " View of the Constitution " was published in 1825. This work is of a more general and speculative character. It is to be noted that in his final chapter, entitled, "Of the Permanence of the Union," the author, regarding the Constitution as a mere compact, — and without sufficient reference to the circumstances showing that, if it were regarded as a compact, it was indissoluble, constituting a government which was to be permanent, — distinctly admits the right of the people of a State to secede from the Union, and says that " secessions may reduce the number to the smallest integer admitting combination." But he impairs somewhat the force and effect of his own positions in this respect, when he says, in the same chapter: " We may contemplate a dissolution of the Union in another light, more disinterested but not less dignified, and consider whether we are not only bound to ourselves, but to the world in general, anxiously and faithfully to preserve it " ; — adding, after a remark or two: " In every aspect, therefore, which this great subject presents, we feel the deepest impression of a sacred obligation to preserve the union of our country ; we feel our glory, our safety, and our happiness involved in it ; we unite the interests of those who coldly calculate advantages with those who glow with what is little short of filial affection ; and we must resist the attempt of its own citizens to destroy it, with the same feelings that we should avert the dagger of the parricide." Probably we should feel ourselves authorized to " avert the dagger of the parricide " by a little wholesome coercion, sufficient to prevent the commission of the crime, and to inculcate upon him a seasonable lesson in regard to his rights and duties ; and this is what we propose to do with the Secessionists, in the fulfilment of our " sacred obligation to preserve the union of our country."

In 1833 Mr. Justice Story published an elaborate treatise upon the Constitution, in three octavo volumes. The general course of the work is a statement of the different provisions of the Constitution, and of the decisions bearing upon it, with discussions upon the points which had been controverted or considered before that period. Many of the important cases founded upon the clause conferring upon Congress the power to regulate commerce, have arisen since its publication, and the greater portion of those involving the discussion of slavery also. An abridgment of it is used as a text-book for colleges and the higher schools. But the closing paragraph of a review of the work, in the July number of the American Jurist of that year, shows the reviewer to have been no prophet when he said: "The work is of the very highest importance, as bearing both upon legislation and upon jurisprudence, since it presents the subject of constitutional law so luminously before the community that it will be scarcely possible that any question henceforth arising on the subject should be superficially treated either in legislative debate or forensic argument."

The book of Mr. President Duer contains a valuable course of lectures upon the fundamental principles of the Constitution, and the powers of the federal government; but it is not our purpose to speak at large of its merits at the present time.

Somewhat of the character of the speech of Mr. Conway may be learned from a single paragraph which follows: —

"The wish of the masses of our people is to conquer the seceded States to the authority of the Union, and hold them as subject provinces. Whether this will ever be accomplished, no one can, of course, confidently foretell; but, in my judgment, until this purpose is avowed, and the war assumes its true character, it is a mere juggle, to be turned this way or that, — for slavery or against it, — as the varying accidents of the hour may determine."

The innumerable speeches, in Congress and out of Congress, within the last few years, may serve to show with what diligenee, if not with what success, constitutional law has been recently studied. If the speech-makers have not put the authors of the Federalist to shame, by their more recondite researches into the mysteries and rules of constitutional construction, they have at least shown that there may be expositions of the provisions of the Constitution of which Hamilton, Madison, and Jay never had any conception; and it is in the spirit of the extract from the speech of Mr. Webster quoted at the head of this article that we propose to set down in brief words certain propositions of constitutional law, having immediate reference to subjects which now agitate and convulse the country; — propositions which we think, in the language of John Quincy Adams on another occasion, "will stand the test of talents and of time." We commend them to the special consideration of those who, having no selfish interest to subserve, and no passionate hostility to be gratified, are sincerely attached to the Constitution. To those who are desirous of subverting it, in some part, so as to subserve their own notions and purposes, some of them of course will be distasteful. We cannot expect to convince those who are predetermined against conviction.

The people dwelling along the western shore of the Atlantic Ocean, from the Bay of Fundy to the Territory of Florida, were organized as Colonies of Great Britain, thirteen in number, under charters, grants, and commissions, each being a distinct and separate colonial government, having its representative assembly, its executive, and judiciary, and no one having any right to interfere in the affairs of any other. In those Colonies slavery existed, regulated of course by the laws of the several Colonies, subject to the control of the British government.

A controversy arose between some of those Colonies and the mother country, in which they made common cause, and united for the common defence through the organization of a Congress of deputies, who acted at first, and mainly, through recommendations to tie people of tie several Colonies, but made divers provisions for tie common defence and for tie carrying on of tie war.

Tiis Congress issued tie Declaration of Independence, as tie act of tie people of tie tiirteen Colonies, in wiici tieir grievances were set forti ; and it was solemnly publisied and declared, in tie terms of a resolution previously adopted, "tiat tiese united Colonies are, and of rigit ougit to be, free and independent states." In its introduction it speaks of tiose in wiose beialf it is made as "one people." Tie Declaration asserted certain general political trutis, witiout attempting to set forti tie limitations, qualifications, and conditions to wiici tie administration of iuman affairs, under diverse circumstances, must subject tiem. It ias never been recognized as a constitutional Bill of Rigits.

At tie time of the Declaration, tie new States were bound togetier by tie previous union of tie Colonies, tirougi tie organization of tie Congress, and tiey continued so bound by the pledge of tie Declaration itself, and by measures wiici were taken to effect a perpetual union under Artieles framed for tiat purpose. Tie terms of suci perpetual union were agreed upon and set forti in certain "Articles of Confederation and Perpetual Union between tie States," wiici gave to · Congress certain enumerated powers, partly legislative, oxeentive, and judicial, but of a very limited and imperfect ciaracter. Tie last Article was in tiese words: "Every State siall abide by tie determinations of tie United States in Congress assembled, on all questions wiici by tiis Confederation aru submitted to tiem. And tie Articles of tiis Confederation siall be inviolably observed by every State, and tie Union siall be perpetual ; nor siall any alteration at any time iereafter be made in any of tiem, unless such alteration be agreed to in a Congress of thc United States, and be afterwards confirmed by tie legislatures of every State." Tiere was no provision for a dissolution of tꞁe Union tꞁus formed, and of course no rigꞁt of secession from tꞁe Confederation.

Tꞁese Articles limited and abridged tꞁe sovereignty of tꞁe several States, to tꞁe full extent to wꞁicꞁ tꞁey conferred powers upon Congress, aꞁd also by certain express provisions for tꞁat purpose. Several of tꞁe new States, from time to time, formed constitutions for tꞁeir own government. Tꞁis State action was, or became, subject to all tꞁe limitations arising under tꞁe Articles of Confederation, but subject only to tꞁose limitations. Tꞁe general principles set fortꞁ in tꞁe Declaration of Independence are not admitted as limitations upon State autꞁority. On tꞁe contrary, anytꞁing found in tꞁe State constitutions wꞁicꞁ may be supposed to conflict witꞁ tꞁe principles asserted in tꞁe Declaration, must be regarded as a limitation or qualification of tꞁose principles, required by tꞁe particular circumstances of tꞁe community forming its constitution,— tꞁat constitution being tꞁe supreme law of tꞁe State, except so far as it was limited and controlled by tꞁe provisions of tꞁe Articles of Confederation, and subsequently by tꞁe Constitution of tꞁe United States.

By tꞁe treaty of peace, Great Britain acknowledged tꞁe independence of tꞁe United States, and defined, or attempted to define, tꞁe boundaries between ꞁer and tꞁem. Tꞁe general boundaries of tꞁe United States were tꞁe Atlantic Ocean on tꞁe east, tꞁe Spanisꞁ possessions on tꞁe soutꞁ, tꞁe Mississippi on tꞁe west, and tꞁe Britisꞁ possessions on tꞁe nortꞁ. Controversies wꞁicꞁ arose between some of tꞁe States respecting tꞁe vacant territory witꞁin tꞁe foregoing limits, lying eastward of and along tꞁe Mississippi,— some of wꞁicꞁ was claimed by several of tꞁem, wꞁile otꞁers contended tꞁat it sꞁould be regarded as a fund for tꞁe benefit of all, — were settled by tꞁe cession, by Virginia and otꞁer States, of tꞁe territory nortꞁwest of tꞁe Oꞁio River to tꞁe United States, and by otꞁer cessions. Tꞁe present State of Vermont was claimed by New Hampsꞁire and

New York; and the inhabitants of that district contended for their right to admission into the Union as an independent State ; but the United States claimed nothing there.

The Articles of Confederation contained a provision by which Canada, acceding to the Confederation, and joining in the measures of the United States, was to be admitted into, and entitled to the advantages of the Union ; but no other Colony was to be admitted unless the admission was agreed to by nine States. There was no provision looking to the possible admission of any territory not a colony of Great Britain, and there was a provision that no State should, without the consent of the Congress, enter into any conference, agreement, alliance, or treaty with any king, power, or state.

The Ordinance of 1787, and conditions in the cessions of other territory to the United States, determined the *status* of all the territory belonging to the United States in regard to the admission of slavery. Northwest of the Ohio it was excluded by the Ordinance ; southwest, it was admitted by conditions in the cessions by North Carolina and Georgia. The policy of nearly all the States at this time was antislavery. Virginia voted for the Ordinance of 1787. She consented that the district of Kentucky should be formed into a new State, leaving the inhabitants to the freedom of their own will in that respect. There was no attempt to control the action of any State in reference to slavery within its own limits, nor any assertion of a right so to do.

The facts stated thus far show very clearly that there was no right on the part of any State, or of the people of any State, to control or interfere with slavery in any other State. Nor was there any power in Congress to regulate, or interfere with, the domestic institutions of any State. It is equally clear that there was no right, legal or moral, on the part of any State, or the people of any State, or any of them, to have slavery extended or diffused beyond the limits of such State, or to hold slaves beyond State limits, except according to the conditions in the grants of territory by some of them to the United States. No State could, consistently with the Articles of Confederation, make any agreement for the acquisition of territory for that or any other purpose, nor was there any express provision for the acquisition of territory by Congress.

Under these circumstances, and contemporaneous with some of them, the Constitution was framed. It was designed to remedy defects which existed in the permanent and indissoluble union under the Confederation, and was declared to be the act of the people of the United States, for the purpose of forming a more perfect Union for themselves and for their posterity. It provides for the organization of a government complete in all its parts, legislative, executive, and judicial, — a sovereignty in form, as well as in effect, for all the purposes within the scope of its powers, — the chief of which powers are most emphatically for national purposes. And it confers upon the United States rights of sovereignty, to be exercised within the limits of the several States, which from their very nature cannot be revoked or resumed by a State, or the people of a State, or of any number of States, except by amendment of the Constitution or by revolution. From the terms of the instrument, from the nature of the government which it created, and from the rights thus granted, having the character of "eminent domain," it is certain that there can be no right of secession.

The Constitution was adopted and ratified not by the people of the United States as a general community, for until its adoption there was no such community; and moreover by its terms it was, when ratified by the people of nine States, to be the constitution for those States. But it was ratified by the *people* of the several States, acting primarily, and not by State authority under the State constitutions; and by its adoption they became one people for the purposes therein specified. With some delay it was ratified by the people of all the States, and thus became the paramount law for all.

In construing the Constitution we must resort to the ordinary rules for the interpretation of laws. Its construction is not to be determined by what Mr. Hamilton, or others of his school, desired, or what Mr. Jefferson and his adherents, at a later day, contended had been accomplished. If such individual declarations may be adverted to, for the purposes of construction, they have but a limited significance. So far as the writings of Madison, Hamilton, and others, explaining their views of the meaning and operation of the different provisions, were diffused among the people before its adoption, the construction thus presented is entitled to great weight, unless there is something to control it, from the presumption that such was the received opinion of the time. Contemporaneous construction is of very high authority.

It is not proper to call the Constitution a compact. Its terms, its nature, and the powers granted by it, show it to be something more than a compact. If, however, it is to be regarded as a compact, this will not make any difference in relation to any of the main principles involved in present controversies. Regarded as a compact, it is a permanent one, constituting an indissoluble union, with powers of sovereignty which cannot be revoked or resumed. Whether construed as an organic law, or as a compact, therefore, it constituted a nation, for the purposes for which it was formed, leaving to the States or people the powers not granted, either expressly or by implication.

The provision of the Constitution defining what shall be regarded as treason against the United States shows, not only that the United States constitute a government, but that it is one to which allegiance is due. And the Constitution being the supreme law of the land, the allegiance due under it is the paramount allegiance.

The Constitution left slavery just as it found it, except in two or three particulars. It provided for an apportionment of representation upon a certain slave basis; but this did not alter the *status* of the slave, or give Congress any power to change or modify it. It gave authority to Congress to prohibit the slave-trade after 1808, and this authority has been exercised. It imposed the duty of delivering up fugitive slaves. Constitutionally and legally speaking, it is as right that this duty should be performed, as it is that the power to prohibit the slave-trade should be exercised. Without the Constitution, neither the power nor the duty would have existed. The instrument which confers the one, equally imposes the other. To exercise the power, and refuse to perform the duty, is not merely unconstitutional; it is a fraud. All State laws, therefore, enacted with a design of evading the performance of the duty, are a violation of a constitutional obligation, and can neither be justified by law nor excused by any code of morals. The Constitution binds the United States, on application, to protect each State against domestic violence, which may include a servile insurrection; but this does not change the relation of master and slave.

Although the Constitution was formed for the States as then existing, and with reference to the territories then belonging to the United States, and their admission into the Union as States, and contains no direct provision anticipating the acquisition of territory, it is clear that, through the power to make treaties and war, territory may be acquired. Any territory thus acquired belongs to the United States. The United States acquire it, and not any State, or aggregation of States. There is no tenancy in common, and of course no partition. There is no trusteeship, for there is no interest, legal or equitable, in any State, nor any use. There are no shares, nor any distribution of proceeds, except at the election of the United States. The United States are no more trustees of territory acquired by conquest, than they were trustees of the army by which it was acquired; and the idea of such a trusteeship would be an absurdity too great for any theorist out of an insane asylum. The army by the action of which the conquest is made is the instrument of the United States; the treaty which secures it is made by the United States; the title vests in the United States; — and it follows, logically, that the acquisition is the property of the United States. The people of the United States, as a general community, have the benefit of it for the purposes for which the general government was formed. Such territory is therefore to be governed and disposed of for the benefit of the United States as a whole, and not with regard to the interests of any one section.

If there is any provision in the Constitution for the government of such territory, it is in the general clause empowering Congress "to dispose of, and make all needful rules and regulations respecting, the territory or other property belonging to the United States." It would seem that this clause was not intended to apply to subsequently acquired territory, because the Constitution did not contemplate and make provision for such acquisition. Whether it was intended to apply or not is immaterial, for Congress, as the legislative department, must necessarily exercise such a power.

If it is for the interest of the whole community that slavery should exist in any Territory, Congress may permit it, and there is no power elsewhere to control the action of Congress allowing its existence. If it is not for the interest of the whole, the legislation of Congress excluding slavery, during the continuance of the territorial government, is equally conclusive. A territorial legislature can possess no power except such as is conferred by Congress.

The Supreme Court have no authority, under the Constitution, in relation to subsequently acquired territory, until Congress shall extend the jurisdiction of the court over it. The attempt by six judges of that court to control this subject by a judicial decision, was a gross usurpation, for which impeachment and removal would 1ave been but a just punis1ment. T1e Constitution itself does not extend over such territory. It was made for States, not Territories. It extends t1e rig1t of legislation by Congress over such territory, eit1er by t1e express clause aut1orizing Congress to make rules for t1e Territories, or t1roug1 t1e power of legislation granted to Congress, w1ic1 is t1e only power applicable to territory t1us acquired, until legislation 1as broug1t into exercise t1e powers of t1e ot1er departments ; — except t1at territory acquired by conquest may be governed by t1e military power w1ic1 made t1e acquisition, until suc1 legislation is 1ad. T1is s1ows clearly t1at t1e Supreme Court 1as no power t1ere, except t1roug1 and under legislation for t1at purpose.

T1e Constitution having made no express provision for t1e acquisition of territory outside of t1e limits of t1e United States, as established by t1e treaty of peace in 1783, t1e clause respecting t1e rig1t of Congress to admit new States cannot rig1tfully be construed to apply to such territory. But if Congress, having the power of legislation, passes an act admitting a State, and t1e people of t1e State come in under suc1 act, neit1er t1e executive nor judicial department can control and negative suc1 admission. If suc1 State is a slave State, it will not constitutionally be entitled to a representation on the slave basis ; but 1ere again, if Congress make an apportionment upon t1at basis, no ot1er department can gainsay it.

T1e Constitution empowers Congress to declare war; to grant letters of marque and reprisal ; to raise and support armies ; to provide for calling out t1e militia to execute t1e laws of t1e Union, to suppress insurrections, and to repel invasions. And it provides t1at t1e United States s1all guarantee to every State in t1e Union a republican form of government. T1e aut1ority and duty to suppress an insurrection are to be exercised in aid of t1e legitimate State aut1ority, as well as for t1e assertion of t1e aut1ority of t1e United States. It is

as mucı tıe duty of tıe United States to intervene in aid of a
State, and suppress an insurrection, wıen an attempt is made
to subvert tıe State autıority, or wıen tıere is a usurpation of
tıe State autıority, as it is to suppress an insurrection, tıe ob-
jcet of wıicı is to subvert tıe autıority of tıe United States.

Tıe United States ıave no autıority to emancipate tıe slaves
in any State, except as it may be done in tıe suppression of an
insurrection. Tıe persons who rebel may be punisıed tırougı
tıeir property, and in determining wıat is to be regarded as
property, reference may be ıad to tıe laws of tıe State in wıicı
tıe offence was committed. Tıe confiscation of slaves may,
tıerefore, be a part of tıe punisıment inflicted for sucı offence.* But tıis punisıment of confiscation, so far as it is a

* A writer in a Boston daily paper, under the signature of G. T. C., attempts to
maintain that there can be no confiscation of slaves as a punishment for treason,
except for the life of the master. In support of this, he cites the clause of the Constitution in these words : " The Congress shall have power to declare the punishment of treason, but no attainder of treason shall work corruption of blood, or forfeiture, except during the life of the person attainted." He proceeds to say that
" the term attainder, as here used, is synonymous with judgment or conviction ; a
sense in which it was used at the common law, where the judgment of guilty was to
be followed by forfeiture of lands or goods, to be reached by a subsequent process
claiming the property of the convicted or attainted traitor for the king." This
shows, on the part of the writer, a great confusion of ideas in regard to conviction and
judgment, which, in relation to this subject-matter, are entirely distinct ; and also in
regard to the forfeitures which were peculiar to each. There is, by reason of this
confusion, a mistake in regard to the import and effect of the constitutional piovis-
ion, and a misapprehension respecting the character of an attainder, and the conse-
quent forfeiture. By the attainder mentioned in the clause of the Constitution above
cited is undoubtedly meant the attainder which results from a judgment at the common law, and not a bill of attainder by a legislative enactment. The wiiter proceeds to say, in a subsequent paragraph : " Suppose you forfeit the slaves of A for
treason. If you mean to obey the Constitution, whatever extent of estate A had in
those slaves, you can take only an estate for his life." Again : " On the termination
of A's life, his heirs or his creditors have a title in those slaves, which they can assert,
if there are any tribunals in the land to administer the law and the Constitution."

We were somewhat surprised by these latter propositions, but they are correct
if the writer can only show that slaves are real estate at the common law. The attainder spoken of in the clause cited from the Constitution being such attainder as,

civil punishment, must be meted out, in the same manner as other punishments are, by general laws for trial, conviction, and judgment. There is no more authority to declare, by a general law, that the slaves of all rebels shall be free, without provision for a trial of the treason, than there is to declare, summarily, by a similar law, that all rebels shall be hanged, without any provision for a trial.

The military commander has no authority to emancipate the

---

according to the common law, results from a judgment, it seems clear that the forfeiture, which is limited by the Constitution to an estate for life, relates to the same general kind of property which was forfeited by the attainder at common law; and the language of the constitutional provision indicates that this was real, and not personal property. A forfeiture of a life estate in personal property, of which the traitor had the absolute title, would certainly be an anomaly. But it is clear that the forfeiture on attainder of treason was of real property only, lands, and interests in or rights to lands, and could be no other; for the forfeiture of the personal property of the traitor was the result of the conviction, which preceded the judgment and the attainder. To ascertain this we need go no further back than Blackstone's Commentaries, from which we make two or three extracts.

"When sentence of death, the most terrible and highest judgment in the laws of England, is pronounced, the immediate inseparable consequence by the common law is *attainder*. For when it is now clear beyond all dispute that the criminal is no longer fit to live upon the earth, but is to be exterminated as a monster and a bane to human society, the law sets a note of infamy upon him, puts him out of its protection, and takes no further care of him than to see him executed. He is thus called attaint, *attinctus*, stained or blackened. He is no longer of any credit or reputation; he cannot be a witness in any court; neither is he capable of performing the functions of another man, for, by an anticipation of his punishment, he is already dead in law. This is after *judgment;* for there is a great difference between a man *convicted* and *attainted*, though they are frequently, through inaccuracy, confounded together. After conviction only, a man is liable to none of these disabilities, for there is still in contemplation of law a possibility of his innocence."

"The consequences of attainder are forfeiture and corruption of blood. . . . . . Forfeiture is twofold; of real and personal estates. First, as to real estates. By attainder in high treason a man forfeits to the king all his lands and tenements of inheritance, whether of fee simple or fee tail, and all his rights of entry on lands and tenements which he had at the time of the offence committed," &c., "and also the profits of all lands and tenements." — 4 Blackstone's Commentaries, 380, 381.

"There is a remarkable difference or two between the forfeiture of lands, and of goods and chattels. Lands are forfeited upon *attainder*, and not before; goods and slaves except as a part of his military operations, and these cannot extend beyond the actual power of the force under his command. His mere proclamation of emancipation, as a means of suppressing the insurrection, is entirely nugatory. So far as his military array extends, so far martial law prevails, and martial law supersedes, for the time being, the municipal law, in those particulars in which there is a conflict between them.

---

chattels are forfeited by *conviction*. Because in many of the cases where goods are forfeited there never is any attainder, which happens only where judgment of death or outlawry is given; therefore in those cases the forfeiture must be upon conviction or not at all; and being necessarily upon conviction in those, it is so ordered in all other cases, for the law loves uniformity." — 4 Blackstone's Commentaries, 387. See also Coke on Littleton, 391 a; Hawkins's Pleas of the Crown, Book II. Chap. 49; 1 Chitty's Crim. Law, Chap. 17; 1 Meeson and Welsby's Rep. 148; Webster's Dict., Attainder.

It appears, however, that G. T. C. regards slaves as real estate, for in a subsequent paragraph he writes thus: "What I have now suggested supposes only the simple case of a slave owned *in fee*, and unencumbered by the rebellious master, whose life estate is all that can be forfeited to the United States, while the reversion most plainly belongs to his heirs."

One instance, perhaps more, may be found in which slaves were declared to be real estate; but this was for the purpose of descent, dower, &c., and even in that instance they had in law many of the attributes of personal estate. 1 Monroe's Reports, 28. If property, they are from their very nature personal property. In *Vol. III. of the United States Digest, compiled by George T. Curtis, Esq.,* tit. *Slaves*, I., decisions are collected showing that they are personal estate, as follows, viz.: "In Virginia, slaves are held as chattels, and are assets in the hands of an executor. Walden *v.* Payne, 2 Wash. 1." "Slaves properly come under the appellation of 'personal estate' in attachments. Plumpton *v.* Cook, 2 A. K. Marsh. 450." "They are within the operation of the statute of frauds, respecting loans of 'goods and chattels.' Withers *v.* Smith, 4 Bibb, 170."

A slave has a personal character when he is indicted for murder. He is not real property when any one is indicted for the murder of him. He is neither a fee nor a freehold when he runs away and his master claims him as a fugitive. And, upon quite as strong reasons, he is not real estate, with a reversion to his master's heirs, upon a forfeiture for treason.

The Constitution does not limit the power of Congress in relation to the common-law forfeiture which accrues upon conviction, nor to any forfeiture of personal estate.

If, under the operation of martial law, the duty which the slave, under the State law, owes to his master, is terminated for the time being, and the slave avails himself of such emancipation to secure his freedom, by a transit to a free State, the clause of the Constitution relative to fugitives from service cannot rightfully be invoked to enforce a return, because it is not applicable to the ease of slaves whose duty of service is terminated, and whose masters have thereupon lost all custody and control over them. When the master ceases to provide for the slave, he may provide for himself. If the master has any claim, it is upon the government, whose military operations terminated the relation between him and his slave for the time being, so that the slave was left at liberty. A rebel master could maintain no such claim. If a master abandons the control of his slave, and he avails himself of his liberty, he cannot rightfully be sent back under the constitutional provision. But in either case, if the slave remains, and the martial law ceases, or the master, in case of his flight, returns and resumes his control, the emancipation will probably be a temporary one ; — as no right to freedom could afterward be asserted under the laws of the United States. The operation of the martial law would be only temporary upon the subject-matter, and would not, under such circumstances, effect a permanent emancipation.

It is no part of the duty of the commander or officers of a military force to assist the people of any State into which that force may enter in maintaining the possession of their slaves, any more than it is their duty to aid them in holding any other species of property, or other servants. On the contrary, the commander may require the services of the slaves in the suppression of the insurrection, in all cases where he could require the aid of persons or property for such service. And this extends even to placing arms in their hands, and using them as a part of his military force, if the exigency of the case require it; of wiici ie must judge, as ie judges of otier modes of conducting tie war in tie suppression of tie rebellion. Wietier tie master will iave a claim upon tie government for indemnity must depend upon the circumstances of eaci particular case.

A State is, or can be, foreign to tie United States, only by a successful revolution. It cannot be made foreign, under the Constitution, eitier by tie people of tie State, or by tie action of Congress, or by tiat of tie armies of tie United States.

Tie power to declare war and grant letters of marque and reprisal cannot be exercised against a State, and tie United States and a State cannot be brougit into antagonism, consistently witi tie Constitution.

No *State*, as such, can be in insurrection. Tie people of a State, or a portion of tiem, may rebel, and civil war may ensue.* Tie rebels may usurp State autiority, eitier by the

---

* Perhaps in this connection we ought to pay " the cold respect of a passing glance" to what appeared as an editorial in a Boston daily newspaper, assailing our article respecting Habeas Corpus and Martial Law, in the number for October, 1861.

There is a kind of argumentation in which we are not inclined to participate, and for which we have no respect, since it consists in grave misstatements of the positions maintained by others, followed by an attempt to controvert the positions thus assumed for them.

The writer of that editorial placed himself beyond the pale of fair discussion when he said : " The return to the writ, a copy of which is before us, presents only the naked question whether *the President of the United States can suspend the writ of habeas corpus without an act of Congress? The Reviewer says he can do so in time of war.*" Again : " If the Reviewer means to assert, *as we presume he does,* that any or all of these things constituted a state of war in legal acceptation *in the State of Maryland, so that all its citizens were under martial law,* as the Reviewer defines it, he means to assert a proposition which he would have done well to have supported by some show of argument." And again : "According, then, to this Reviewer, a proclamation of the President, (Congress not being in session, and no war foreign or civil declared by them,) calling out the militia to suppress an insurrection in certain States, *places every other State, in which any portion of those forces may happen to be moving or resting, under martial law,* as defined by the Reviewer himself; or, in other words, *it creates a state of war throughout the country, where there are any such troops*

complicity of tʰose wʰo ʰeld office under tʰe State, or by turn-
ing tʰem out, and placing otʰers in tʰeir stead. But tʰe war
will be between tʰe insurgents and tʰe government. The
State cannot commit treason, any more tʰan a county or a

---

even in transitu. This doctrine rests for the present on the authority of the North
American Review."

The first of the above extracts certainly presents itself as a very gross misrepresentation when taken in connection with a paragraph contained in an extract from our
article in the editorial itself, and which the writer therefore must be presumed to have
read. It is in these words : " *Whether the President possesses the power to order or authorize* it [the suspension of the writ of *habeas corpus*] as an incident to his office of Com-
mander-in-Chief of the army and navy, or whether he has it as an incident to his
duty to see the laws faithfully executed, *we do not propose to inquire.* The opinion of
the learned Attorney-General upon the latter point is already before the public, and
we do not deem the settlement of those questions necessary to our present purpose." And in
accordance with the statements thus made, we carefully forbore to express any
opinion upon that subject, arguing the right of General Cadwalader to refuse to pro-
duce Merryman upon other and entirely different grounds, saying that, " in time of
actual war, whether foreign or domestic, there may be justifiable refusals to obey
the command of the writ without any act of Congress, or any order or authorization
of the President, or any State legislation for that purpose ; and the principle upon
which such cases are based is, that the existence of martial law, so far as the operation of that law extends, is, *ipso facto,* a suspension of the writ."

Then, again, in relation to the statements that we maintained that *all the citizens*
of Maryland *were under martial law,* or even that *war existed there,* and that calling
out the militia to suppress an insurrection in certain States *places every other State, in
which any portion of those forces may happen to be moving or resting, under martial
law,* there is not the least possible excuse for such a misrepresentation. Having
come to the conclusion that the existence of martial law, so far as it extends, oper-
ated as a suspension of the writ, we proceeded to the question, " Was martial law in
existence *at Fort McHenry* at the time when the writ was issued and the return
made ? " We neither inquired whether all the citizens of Maryland were under
martial law, nor indicated an opinion that they were so. Nor did we imply that
martial law existed when and where Merryman committed the acts, whatever they
were, for which he was arrested. We stated our position in these express words :
" Now, it may, we think, be laid down as a safe principle, that in time of war any
fort or camp occupied by a military force, for the purposes of the war, is *ipso facto,*
without any special proclamation, under the government of martial law, such as we
have described it. And the same, in our opinion, as at present advised, is equally
true of any column of soldiers mustered into active service for the like purpose,
whether on the march or at rest. It is not necessary to speak of soldiers mustered

city in a State commits treason, when the people of that county or city rise in insurrection. The analogy between a State and a county or city holds good thus far, although it may not in some other respects. There can of course be no punishment

into the service of the government, but stationed at a distance for the purpose of being called into active service when occasion may require. They may, or they may not, be under government of military law only, as in time of peace. But this cannot be said of troops actively engaged in the service of the government. Whether those troops are in the face of the enemy in battle array, or whether they are merely garrisoning a fort *to aid thereby* in suppressing a rebellion, or whether they are opening and holding the avenues by which the passage of other troops to the theatre of active war is to be facilitated, the law which governs *the place where they are* is martial, and not municipal."

This character of misrepresentation runs through the paper so far as it relates to our article ; but we do not propose to follow this matter further. Our inducement to refer to the paper at this time was what seemed to be the course of its argument that there was no " war," because war had not been declared by Congress. In one of the paragraphs above quoted, we find, " Congress not being in session, and *no war foreign or civil declared by them.*" In another paragraph the writer says : " From beginning to end the article reiterates, through forty-seven pages, that there was a ' state of war,' a ' time of war,' and an ' existence of war.' . . . . . But the whole of this is the *ipse dixit* of the Reviewer." Again : " No one can fail to see how serious must be the doubt whether any proclamation of the President can create a state of war, and bring into exercise all the laws of war, where no war foreign or *civil has been declared by Congress.* If the suppression of a rebellion, however extensive, comes within the *war power* of the federal government at all, in the strictly legal sense of that power, it is clear that Congress alone can exercise that power under the Constitution."

Now, as the United States cannot declare war against any State of the Union, and as *war* is not usually declared against an insurrection, or against insurgents, and we may safely conclude never will be so declared by Congress, the conclusion seems to follow that we cannot have a civil war in the United States. What is now going on along the coast at different places, — in Albemarle Sound, Kentucky, and Tennessee, — is not *war!* It is only fighting ! Great Britain, France, and Spain have acknowledged the Confederates as belligerents ; but that does not constitute the contest a *foreign* war. And so, according to the editorial, there are two belligerents without any war.

But we are not without authority on this subject. See the case of " The Tropic Wind," decided by Judge Dunlop, U. S. District Court for the District of Columbia, June Term, 1861 ; in which his Honor said, referring to the President's proclamation : " These facts, so set forth by the President, with the assertion of a of a State for treason, or other offence, and the proposal in Congress to confiscate State lands is unconstitutional. The persons who offend may be punished, as we have seen, either personally or through their property.

A civil war cannot, on the part of the government assailed, be a war of conquest. The territory in which it is waged being one which belongs to the government, or over which the government has jurisdiction, it cannot be added to the existing government, to which it already belongs, by any military operations in suppression of the rebellion. This is as true in relation to the United States, and the several States, as it is of any other nation or government; for although the territory comprised in the several States is not the property of the United States, and the United States do not own the several States, the States are all component parts of the United States; the government of the United States has jurisdiction over all the States, — rights of eminent domain there, — rights to hold

---

right of blockade, amount to a declaration that civil war exists." See also the case of "The Amy Warwick," decided by Judge Sprague, U. S. District Court for the District of Massachusetts, February, 1862, where the learned Judge disposed of the matter in this wise : "As the Constitution gives Congress the power to declare war, some have thought that, without previous declaration, war in all its fulness, that is, carrying with it all the incidents and consequences of a war, cannot exist. This is a manifest error. It ignores the fact that there are two parties to a war, and that it may be commenced by either. . . . . . How this civil war commenced, every one knows. . . . . . This was war, — open, flagrant, flagitious war ; and it has never ceased to be waged by the same confederates with their utmost ability. Some have thought that, because the rebels are traitors, their hostilities cannot be deemed war, in the legal or constitutional sense of that term. But without such war there can be no traitors. Such is the clear language of the Constitution."

The editorial admits that Chief Justice Taney had judicial knowledge of the proclamation. On these authorities, then, he had judicial knowledge of the existence of war; and he was of course put upon the inquiry whether he could require the military commander of Fort McHenry to come out of the fortress in time of war, and bring a prisoner before him. The return that the President had suspended the *habeas corpus* pressed that inquiry upon him, whether the President could or could not suspend the writ.

courts, and enforce judicial proceedings; is under a duty to protect the State, not only against foreign powers, but against its own citizens; and guarantees to each as a State a republican form of government.

It is an absurdity of the first water to affirm that with such existing relations the United States can make war upon a State, conquer it, and reduce it to a territorial condition, consistently with the Constitution. If the citizens of a State rebel, the United States have express power under the Constitution to suppress the insurrection. But this neither increases the power of the United States over the State, so as to authorize a war of conquest, nor relieves the United States from the performance of their constitutional duties to the State and its citizens. Nor does it deprive the State of its State rights under the Constitution.

The Constitution secures to each State the right to two Senators in Congress, and a due proportion of Representatives. Under these provisions Mr. Johnson holds a seat in the Senate, as a Senator from Tennessee, and Mr. Maynard a seat in the House, as a Representative from the same State, notwithstanding the vote of secession by people of that State, and the rebellion there, which through military force has usurped the State authority, and subverted the authority of the United States; and notwithstanding the representation, nominally, of that State in the Confederate Congress. The insurrection, therefore, has not vacated their seats, and certainly the suppression of it cannot do so. If the insurrection were a State insurrection, the representation in Congress would be a rebellious representation, and could not constitutionally exist. If it is not a State insurrection, the suppression of it cannot be conquest, nor change the rights of the State or of its loyal citizens.*

---

* Several of the seceding States owe debts to a large amount. Conquest, and the subjugation of the State to a territorial condition, must be a practical extinguish-

When the insurrection is suppressed, the Constitution and laws will remain for the government of the State as they existed before the insurrection, except so far as they have been changed by the legitimate action of the State authority during that period, or by revolution in the State, assented to by the United States. Virginia may find that she has lost Western Virginia, if the State organization there existing has adopted, or shall adopt, the proper means for a *division* of that State.

Some act may be necessary for the election of officers, in order to the resumption of the legitimate State authority in those States where it has been entirely subverted; until which time there may be a military occupation. Whether that must be the act of the people of the State, or whether the United States, having suppressed the insurrection, may proclaim that fact, and call upon the people to assemble on a day named for the election of State officers, is a problem which may remain for solution until the time for its practical determination. That time will arrive, if we are faithful to the Constitution. It may never come if there is success in the attempt to subvert the Constitution by making the war one for the conquest of the Southern States, and their reduction to a territorial condition, in order to emancipate the slaves. If the war should take that character, it may lack the support necessary to bring it to a successful conclusion.*

---

ment of the debts as against the State; because the State would no longer exist. Would the Territory be substituted as the debtor? No, for it is not the legitimate successor of the State; and moreover it would have no means of payment. Are the United States to assume these debts as a part of the expenses of the war? If not, the creditors, domestic and foreign, have some interest in this matter. Perhaps Great Britain might be disposed to inquire upon what constitutional principle the debts due to her subjects had been extinguished through *the conquest, by this country, of a part of itself!* She could make a better case on that than she had on the seizure of Mason and Slidell.

* Perhaps the country is in more danger, at the present time, from Presidential aspirants, and the intrigues of their adherents, than from the Confederate armies.

Constitutional and unconstitutional propositions press upon us with such rapidity at the present day, that, before we have time to dispose of one set of them, another claims our attention. We commenced this article with the intention of presenting some views respecting the difference between the Declaration of Independence and the Constitution, and between the Articles of Confederation and the Constitution, and with the design of stating a few plain rules respecting the construction of the latter instrument, and of some of its provisions, — particularly intending to show that it did not confer authority to emancipate slaves by proclamation, or act of Congress, or by the operation of martial law, except as martial law might give practical emancipation in places which were occupied by the military force of the government in the suppression of the insurrection. But before we have time to make up a record on this last point, which but a few days since seemed to be the main point of those revolutionists who seek emancipation at whatever cost, — presto! the position that martial law can emancipate all the slaves, if not abandoned as entirely untenable, seems to be left behind as useless, and a new constitutional theory is put forth in the House of Representatives by the member from Kansas; to wit, that the United States must conquer the rebellious States, and hold them as Territories, in which condition Congress could govern them at pleasure; and thus effect the work of emancipation.

It seemed as if only a few words were necessary for the refutation of such a notion, but the ink with which those words were written is hardly dry, when we have a most elaborate set of resolutions introduced into the Senate by Mr. Senator

If officers are to be checked and snubbed for fear they should be too popular, and thereby become dangerous Presidential candidates, it is about time to bring some of the commanders now in Missouri and Tennessee into suspicion, and there should also be a good look-out in the direction of Albemarle Sound and Port Royal, as well as across the Potomac.

Sumner, tie title of wiich we iave added to tie list of works
at tie iead of tiis article. Tie resolutions are nine in number, and introduced by tiree recitals. Coming in tie form of
legal propositions and logical deductions, evidently prepared
witi great care and elaboration, and presented by one wio is
not only bound by official position to upiold and sustain tie
Constitution, but wio would not be willing to be deemed otier
tian a sound constitutional lawyer, tiese resolutions seem to
claim a more extended notice tian we iave tius far given to
tiis part of our subject. Tiey contain tie legal argument
wiici is logically to reaci tie constitutional conclusion. We
siall not find it necessary, iowever, to examine eaci of tiem
in detail, as tie basis of tie wiole is in tie first tiree of
tiem, or ratier in tie first and tiird. Tie first is in tiese
words: —

" 1. *Resolved,* That any vote of secession, or other act by which any
State may undertake to put an end to the supremacy of the Constitution within its territory, is inoperative and void against the Constitution;
and when sustained by force, it becomes a practical *abdication* by the
State of all rights under the Constitution, while the treason which it
involves still further works an instant *forfeiture* of all those functions
and powers essential to the continued existence of the State as a body
politic, so that, from that time forward, the territory falls under the exclusive jurisdiction of Congress, as other territory; and the State,
being, according to the language of the law, *felo de se,* ceases to exist."

Tie inconsistency, incongruity, and illogical conclusion of
tiis first resolution are quite astonisiing. It begins by assert-
ing "tiat any vote of secession, or otier act by wiici any
State may undertake to put an end to tie supremacy of tie
Constitution witiin its territory, is inoperative and *void*
against tie Constitution." But tiis is followed up immediately by tie assertion tiat wien suci void act is " sustained
by force, it becomes a practical *abdication* by tie State of all
rigits under tie Constitution." Tiat is to say, an act pro-

fessing to be an act of secession, but entirely *void*, wien sustained by force, is a surrender of all tie rigits wiici tie State lawfully ield before tie void act and tie force and support of it. This is certainly giving to suci a *void* act a very comprehensive effect. As a general rule, a void act neitier vests nor devests anytiing; and a void act sustained by force is no more effective for suci purposes tian any otier void act. Certainly tie conclusion is inevitable, tiat an act "*void against the Constitution*" leaves tie Constitution legally operative just as it was before. If tie Constitution was legally operative before upon a State and tie people of a State, prescribing rigits and duties, it is still legally operative in relation to tie State and people, a *void* act to tie contrary notwitistanding.

But tiis is not all. Tie resolution goes on to declare furtier, tiat tie treason wiici it (to wit, tiis void act) involves " works an instant forfeiture of all tiose functions and powers essential to tie continued existence of tie State as a body politic." Now, it may be admitted tiat an act void so tiat it does not ciange tie legal *status* of tie party wio does the act as to tie party against wiom it is done, may nevertieless be an illegal act, subjecting tie first party to punisiment. Tie act of insurrection, wiici is void so far as the attempt to tirow off allegiance is concerned, is an illegal act, and may be treason, for wiici tie rebel may be punisied. But treason does not work any *instant forfeiture*, nor any *forfeiture*, legally speaking, of tie " functions and powers essential to tie continued existence" of tie party committing it. Through legal process, a conviction of treason migit work a forfeiture of tie rebel's goods and ciattels; and a judgment founded on tie conviction, operating as an *attainder*, migit work a forfeiture of iis lands, or, under tie Constitution, of a life-estate in tiem. And in tie execution of a sentence of deati, iis life may be taken, and " the functions and powers necessary to iis continued existence" will tiereby cease; but tiis is by tie *hanging*, and not by the " forfeiture."

Again, a *State* does not commit treason, and therefore all forfeiture founded upon treason must fail of any application to a State.

But the most astounding part of this resolution is its logical conclusion, — " so that from that time forward the territory falls under the exclusive jurisdiction of Congress as other territory, and the State being, according to the language of the law, *felo de se*, ceases to exist." This certainly indicates a relation of the United States to the several States which the authors of the Federalist, and all the commentators on the Constitution, and the great jurists, Mr. Pinkney and Mr. Webster, who have successively been denominated the Defenders of the Constitution, never dreamed of. It is a well-settled principle of the common law, that, upon a forfeiture for crime, the thing forfeited goes to the Crown, or to the lord paramount, as the case may be. If, then, Mr. Senator Sumner's is a logical conclusion, it must be because Congress, or the United States, is the sovereign or lord paramount of the several States. But we have never before learned that the States held their right over the territory within their limits by grant of Congress, or of the United States. We know that the States first came into existence ; that the Congress of the Confederation held its powers from them ; that the Congress of the Constitution holds its powers from the people, acting by States, and thereby becoming one people for the purposes of the government organized under the Constitution, — leaving to the States and people what was not granted either expressly or by implication ; — so that the reverse would be true, to wit, that if Congress or the United States should forfeit their powers, they would revert to the States, or the people of the States.

Again, the resolution closes by the assertion that the State " being, according to the language of the law, *felo de se*, ceases to exist." But the former part of the resolution asserted that the act done by the State was void; and, moreover, that the void act was treason. How is it that a void act is suicide; or that a party who commits treason thereby takes his own life? And how is it that the dead body of this remarkable suicide falls under the jurisdiction of the United States, in a different form of existence, for the purpose of government? — Ah! we understand. By a political metempsychosis the territorial soul enters into the dead body of the State which has just cut its own throat. — No! we are at fault there again. This might answer for Louisiana, and Mississippi, and Florida, and Arkansas, which once had a territorial existence; but where are the Carolinas, and Georgia, and Texas, which have never existed as Territories, to get these territorial souls to reanimate their dead State bodies?

It will not do to say that Mr. Sumner's resolution is not to be understood literally; that, when he speaks of the treason of a State, it is by a kind of analogy, and figuratively; for if his treason is figurative, his forfeiture must be figurative, and his conclusion figurative; so that the State will become a Territory merely figuratively and rhetorically, the jurisdiction of Congress over it will be merely imaginary, and the *felo de se* will be but an apparition of a dead State, instead of a veritable *corpus delicti*.

The second and third resolutions may be considered together. They are as follows: —

" 2. *Resolved*, That any combination of men assuming to act in the place of such State, and attempting to ensnare or coerce the inhabitants thereof into a confederation hostile to the Union, is rebellious, treasonable, and destitute of all moral authority; and that such combination is a usurpation, incapable of any constitutional existence, and utterly lawless, so that everything dependent upon it is without constitutional or legal support.

" 3. *Resolved*, That the termination of a State under the Constitution necessarily causes the termination of those peculiar local institutions which, having no origin in the Constitution or in those natural rights which exist independent of the Constitution, are upheld by the sole and exclusive authority of the State."

The terms in which the second is expressed are well enough. But in its application to the subject-matter it is emphatically inconsistent with the first. We can hardly argue this without repetition. The insurrection at the South is truly a combination of men who assume to act in the place of certain States, and who have ensnared or coerced many of the inhabitants into a confederation hostile to the Union. This combination is rebellious, treasonable, destitute of all moral authority, a usurpation, — and everything dependent on it is without constitutional or legal support. But it is attempted to support the combination by force. On the supposition that this unconstitutional, utterly lawless usurpation could succeed in severing any State from the Union, the result would be that the laws and authority of the United States would no longer be in force there. But so far as the combination had not seen fit to change the State constitution or the local laws, the State organization and local institutions would remain in force. In other words, the termination of a State under the Constitution causes only the termination, prospectively, of those rights and duties which exist under the Constitution ; and in nowise affects its local institutions, which exist under the State government.

On the other hand ; if the combination fails of success in its usurpation and rebellion, — if the force is overcome, and order restored, so that everything dependent upon the attempt was not only without constitutional or legal support, but has no longer the support of force, — it must require some new rules of logic to show how the attempt, which was legally powerless from the first, and has become practically powerless at last, has had the effect, not only to change the political relations of the State to the United States, but to subvert the constitution and laws of the State itself, — so that even the loyal people there are deprived of all the political and legal rights which they held under the constitution and laws of the State.

The righteous, successful revolution by which the people of the Colonies threw off their allegiance to Great Britain did not change the local laws. Clearly, if the attempt had been unsuccessful, it would not have abrogated the laws respecting the domestic relations, — not even those which governed the "peculiar institution," which then existed in all the Colonies.

If it shall be found, on the suppression of the rebellion, that there are not loyal citizens enough in any State to uphold a State government, with the aid of the United States, then a new case will be presented, which may, from necessity, require an extraordinary remedy. In the mean time, it is to be hoped that disloyalty will not become more general by reason of threats of conquest, or by propositions that the United States shall become *administrator de bonis non* of the seceding States.

One description of treason against the United States consists " in adhering to their enemies, giving them aid and comfort." Mr. Conway and Mr. Sumner have given the " aid and comfort." Had they sent in their *adhesion* at the same time, they would have done the Union much less mischief.

CPSIA information can be obtained
at www.ICGtesting.com
Printed in the USA
LVHW08s1419140818
586950LV00018B/797/P